Cozy Winter Knitting

Unraveling DIY Projects Book for Ultimate Creativity

Doyle N Radley

THIS BOOK BELONGS TO

The Library of

....

....

I can't tell you how grateful I am that you decided to read my book. My most heartfelt thanks that you took time out of your life to choose my work and I hope you find benefit within these pages.

There are so many books available today that offer similar content so that makes it even more humbling that you decided to buying mine.

Tell me what you thought! I am eager to hear your opinion and ideas on what you read as are others who are looking for a good book to buy. Leave a review on Amazon.com so others can benefit from your wisdom!

With much thanks.

Table of Contents

SUMMARY

What is The Knitting: The Knitting is a popular and versatile craft that involves creating fabric by interlocking loops of yarn or thread using knitting needles or a knitting machine. It is a technique that has been practiced for centuries and has evolved over time to become a beloved hobby for many people around the world.

The process of knitting involves manipulating the yarn or thread with the knitting needles to create various stitches, which are then combined to form a pattern or design. The basic stitches in knitting include the knit stitch and the purl stitch, which are used to create different textures and patterns in the fabric. By combining these stitches in different ways, knitters can create a wide range of items, from simple scarves and hats to intricate sweaters and blankets.

One of the great things about knitting is its versatility. It can be done with a wide variety of materials, including different types of yarn, thread, and even wire. This allows knitters to experiment with different textures, colors, and thicknesses to create unique and personalized pieces. Additionally, knitting can be done by people of all ages and skill levels, making it a great activity for both beginners and experienced crafters.

Knitting is not only a creative outlet, but it also offers numerous benefits for the knitter. It is a relaxing and meditative activity that can help reduce stress and anxiety. The repetitive motions of knitting can have a calming effect on the mind and body, similar to other forms of mindfulness practices. Knitting can also improve hand-eye coordination and fine motor skills, as it requires precise movements and control of the knitting needles.

Furthermore, knitting allows for self-expression and individuality. With countless patterns and designs available, knitters can choose to follow a pattern or create their own unique designs. This allows for a sense of accomplishment and pride in the finished product. Knitting can also be a social activity, as many people enjoy knitting in groups or joining knitting circles to share tips, patterns, and stories.

In addition to being a hobby, knitting has a rich history and cultural significance. It has been practiced by various cultures around the world for centuries, with different regions having their own unique knitting traditions and techniques. Knitted garments have also played a role in fashion and clothing throughout history, with iconic designs such as the Aran sweater and Fair Isle patterns becoming timeless classics.

In conclusion, knitting is a versatile and enjoyable craft that offers numerous benefits for the knitter. Whether you are a beginner or an experienced knitter, there is always something new to learn

Understanding the Transformative Power of Handmade Items in Knitting: In today's fast-paced and technology-driven world, it is easy to overlook the transformative power of handmade items. However, in the realm of knitting, this power is undeniable. Knitting is not just a hobby or a craft; it is a form of self-expression, a means of relaxation, and a way to connect with others.

When we think of knitting, we often envision a cozy sweater or a warm scarf. While these finished products are undoubtedly beautiful and practical, the true power of knitting lies in the process itself. The act of knitting requires focus, patience, and creativity. As we loop yarn around needles and create intricate patterns, we enter a state of flow, where time seems to stand still and our worries fade away.

This meditative quality of knitting is what makes it so transformative. In a world filled with constant distractions and stress, knitting provides a much-needed escape. It allows us to slow down, to be present in the moment, and to find solace in the repetitive motion of our hands. As we knit, we become more attuned to our thoughts and emotions, and we gain a deeper understanding of ourselves.

Furthermore, knitting is a powerful tool for self-expression. With each stitch, we are able to create something unique and personal. Whether it is a vibrant blanket or a delicate lace shawl, our knitting projects reflect our individual tastes and preferences. Through our choice of colors, textures, and patterns, we are able to convey our personality and tell our own stories.

But knitting is not just a solitary activity. It is also a means of connecting with others. Knitting circles and groups have long been a source of community and support. In these gatherings, knitters come together to share their passion, exchange ideas, and offer encouragement. The act of knitting becomes a shared experience, fostering a sense of belonging and camaraderie.

Moreover, the act of gifting a handmade knitted item holds a special significance. When we give someone a knitted scarf or a pair of socks, we are not just giving them a physical object; we are giving them a piece of ourselves. We are saying, I took the time and effort to create something just for you. This act of giving is not only a demonstration of love and care, but it also creates a lasting bond between the giver and the recipient.

How to Utilize This Guide to Master Knitting and Complete Projects: Welcome to our comprehensive guide on mastering knitting and completing projects! Whether you are a beginner or an experienced knitter looking to enhance your skills, this guide is designed to provide you with all the necessary information and techniques to become a knitting expert.

To make the most of this guide, it is important to approach it with a systematic and organized mindset. Here are some steps you can follow to effectively utilize this guide and achieve your knitting goals:

1. Familiarize Yourself with the Basics: Start by understanding the fundamental concepts of knitting. Learn about different types of yarns, knitting needles, and essential knitting tools. Familiarize yourself with basic knitting stitches such as the knit stitch and the purl stitch. Practice these stitches until you feel comfortable and confident in your abilities.

2. Learn New Techniques: Once you have a solid foundation in the basics, it's time to expand your repertoire of knitting techniques. This guide will introduce you to various advanced stitches, such as cables, lace, and colorwork. Each technique will be explained in detail, accompanied by step-by-step instructions and helpful illustrations. Take your time to practice and master each technique before moving on to the next one.

3. Explore Different Projects: Knitting is a versatile craft that allows you to create a wide range of items. This guide will provide you with project ideas for different skill levels, from simple scarves and hats to intricate sweaters and blankets. Choose projects that align with your skill level and interests. As you progress, challenge yourself by attempting more complex projects to further enhance your knitting skills.

4. Follow the Instructions: Throughout this guide, you will find detailed instructions for each technique and project. It is crucial to read and understand these instructions thoroughly before starting any project. Pay attention to specific stitch patterns, gauge requirements, and finishing techniques. Following the instructions accurately will ensure that your projects turn out as intended.

5. Practice, Practice, Practice: Like any skill, knitting requires practice to improve. Set aside dedicated time for knitting regularly. Practice the techniques you have learned and experiment with different yarns and patterns. Don't be discouraged by mistakes or setbacks; they are part of the learning process. Embrace them as opportunities to grow and refine your skills.

6. Seek Support and Inspiration: Joining a knitting community or taking part in knitting classes can provide valuable support and inspiration. Interacting with fellow knitters allows you to exchange ideas, troubleshoot problems, and gain insights from experienced individuals. Additionally, explore online

Unraveling the World of Knitting: Tools, Yarn, and Basics:

Unraveling the World of Knitting: Exploring the Tools, Yarn, and Basics of this Timeless Craft

Knitting is a timeless craft that has been passed down through generations, allowing individuals to create beautiful and functional pieces of clothing, accessories, and home decor. Whether you are a beginner or an experienced knitter, understanding the tools, yarn, and basics of knitting is essential to embark on this creative journey.

When it comes to knitting, having the right tools is crucial. The most basic tool is the knitting needle, which comes in various sizes and materials. Straight needles are commonly used for flat knitting, while circular needles are versatile and can be used for both flat and circular knitting. Double-pointed needles are ideal for knitting in the round, such as socks or hats. Additionally, a crochet hook is handy for fixing mistakes or adding decorative elements to your knitting.

Yarn selection is another important aspect of knitting. Yarns come in different weights, which determine the thickness of the yarn. The weight of the yarn you choose will depend on the project you have in mind. For example, a bulky weight yarn is perfect for cozy winter sweaters, while a fingering weight yarn is ideal for delicate lace shawls. Furthermore, the fiber content of the yarn can greatly impact the final result of your knitting. Common yarn fibers include wool, cotton, acrylic, and blends of various fibers. Each fiber has its own unique characteristics, such as warmth, softness, or durability, so it's important to consider these factors when selecting your yarn.

Before diving into complex knitting patterns, it's essential to grasp the basics of knitting. The two fundamental stitches in knitting are the knit stitch and the purl stitch. These stitches create the foundation for various knitting patterns and textures. Learning how to cast on, which is the process of creating the first row of stitches, and how to bind off, which is the process of finishing your knitting, are also essential skills to master. Additionally, understanding how to increase and decrease stitches will allow you to shape your knitting and create intricate designs.

As you delve deeper into the world of knitting, you will discover a plethora of techniques and patterns to explore. From cables and lace to colorwork and intarsia, the possibilities are endless. Knitting not only provides a creative outlet but also offers a sense of accomplishment as you see your project come to life stitch by stitch.

A Guide to Different Yarns, Needles, and Basic Supplies of Knitting: A Comprehensive Guide to Understanding and Choosing the Right Yarns, Needles, and Basic Supplies for Knitting

Introduction:

Knitting is a popular craft that allows individuals to create beautiful and functional items using yarn and needles. However, for beginners, the wide variety of yarns, needles, and other supplies available can be overwhelming. This guide aims to provide a comprehensive overview of different yarns, needles, and basic supplies used in knitting, helping you make informed choices and enhance your knitting experience.

Yarns:

Yarn is the fundamental material used in knitting, and understanding its different characteristics is crucial for achieving desired results. Yarns can be categorized based on their fiber content, weight, and texture.

1. Fiber Content:

Yarns can be made from various fibers, including wool, cotton, acrylic, silk, and blends. Each fiber has its unique properties, affecting the final appearance, feel, and care requirements of the knitted item. For example, wool yarns are warm and elastic, making them ideal for winter garments, while cotton yarns are breathable and lightweight, suitable for summer projects.

2. Weight:

Yarn weight refers to the thickness of the yarn strand and is classified into categories such as lace, fingering, sport, worsted, and bulky. The weight of the yarn determines the size of the needles to be used and the overall look and drape of the finished piece. Lighter weight yarns are suitable for delicate projects like lace shawls, while heavier weight yarns are ideal for cozy blankets or sweaters.

3. Texture:

Yarn texture refers to the surface characteristics of the yarn, such as smooth, fluffy, or textured. Textured yarns can add visual interest and dimension to your knitting, while smooth yarns are great for showcasing intricate stitch patterns. It's important to consider the texture of the yarn in relation to the desired outcome of your project.

Needles:

Choosing the right needles is essential for comfortable and efficient knitting. Needles come in various materials, lengths, and sizes, each offering different benefits.

1. Material:

Knitting needles can be made from materials like wood, metal, bamboo, and plastic. Each material has its unique feel and properties. For example, wooden needles provide warmth and a natural grip, while metal needles offer smoothness and durability. It's a matter of personal preference and the type of yarn you're working with.

Setting Up Your Knitting Space and Organizing Materials in Knitting: Setting up your knitting space and organizing your materials is an essential step in ensuring a smooth and enjoyable knitting experience. By creating a well-organized and functional space, you can easily access your tools and materials, minimize distractions, and maximize your productivity.

Firstly, consider the location of your knitting space. Choose a quiet and well-lit area in your home where you can comfortably sit and work for extended periods. Natural light is ideal, as it allows you to see your stitches and colors accurately. If natural light is limited, invest in good quality task lighting to ensure optimal visibility.

Next, think about the furniture and storage options for your knitting space. A comfortable chair with proper back support is crucial to prevent strain and fatigue during long knitting sessions. Additionally, a sturdy table or desk will provide a stable surface for your knitting projects. Consider the size of your projects and the amount of space you need to work comfortably.

When it comes to organizing your knitting materials, having a designated storage system is key. Start by sorting your yarn stash. Group similar types of yarn together, such as wool, cotton, or acrylic, and organize them by color or weight. This will make it easier to find the perfect yarn for your projects. Consider using clear plastic bins or baskets to store your yarn, as they allow you to see the contents at a glance.

In addition to yarn, you'll need to organize your knitting needles and other tools. Invest in a needle case or roll to keep your needles organized and prevent them from getting tangled. You can also use small pouches or containers to store your stitch markers, tapestry needles, and other accessories. Keeping these items organized and easily accessible will save you time and frustration when you need them.

To further enhance your knitting space, consider adding some additional tools and accessories. A yarn swift and ball winder can help you quickly wind skeins of yarn into neat and manageable balls. A blocking mat and pins are essential for blocking and shaping your finished projects. And don't forget to have a notebook or journal handy to keep track of your patterns, notes, and ideas.

Finally, don't forget to personalize your knitting space to make it truly your own. Add some decorative touches, such as artwork, plants, or a cozy blanket, to create a warm and inviting atmosphere. Surrounding yourself with things that inspire and bring you joy will enhance your knitting experience and make it even more enjoyable.

Learning the Knit and Purl Stitches: Learning the knit and purl stitches is an essential skill for anyone interested in knitting. These two basic stitches form the foundation of countless knitting patterns and techniques. Whether you're a beginner or an experienced knitter looking to expand your skills, mastering the knit and purl stitches is a great place to start.

The knit stitch is the most fundamental stitch in knitting. It creates a smooth, v-shaped fabric that is commonly seen in sweaters, scarves, and blankets. To knit, you insert the right-hand needle into the front of the stitch on the left-hand needle, wrap the yarn around the right-hand needle, and pull it through the stitch, sliding the old stitch off the left-hand needle. This process is repeated for each stitch across the row.

The purl stitch, on the other hand, creates a bumpy, textured fabric. It is the reverse of the knit stitch and is often used to create ribbing, seed stitch, and other decorative patterns. To purl, you insert the right-hand needle into the front of the stitch on the left-hand needle, but instead of wrapping the yarn around the needle, you bring it in front of the work. Then, you insert the right-hand needle into the back of the stitch on the left-hand needle, wrap the yarn around the right-hand needle, and pull it through the stitch, sliding the old stitch off the left-hand needle. This process is repeated for each stitch across the row.

Learning these two stitches opens up a world of possibilities in knitting. Once you have mastered the basics, you can combine knit and purl stitches in various ways to create different patterns and textures. For example, you can create stockinette stitch by knitting one row and purling the next, resulting in a smooth fabric on one side and a bumpy fabric on the other. You can also create ribbing by alternating knit and purl stitches in a specific pattern, which is commonly used for cuffs, collars, and hems.

In addition to their versatility, the knit and purl stitches are also relatively easy to learn. With a little practice, you can quickly develop a rhythm and consistency in your knitting. As you become more comfortable with these stitches, you can experiment with different yarns, needle sizes, and stitch patterns to create unique and personalized projects.

There are numerous resources available to help you learn the knit and purl stitches. Online tutorials, knitting books, and local knitting groups are all great places to start.

Understanding Gauge, Tension, and Reading Patterns in Knitting:

Knitting is a popular craft that allows individuals to create beautiful and functional items using yarn and needles. However, to achieve the desired outcome, it is crucial to understand and master certain concepts such as gauge, tension, and reading patterns.

Gauge refers to the number of stitches and rows per inch in a knitted fabric. It is essential to match the gauge specified in a knitting pattern to ensure that the finished item will have the correct dimensions. To determine gauge, knitters typically create a swatch by knitting a small sample using the recommended yarn and needle size. The swatch is then measured to determine the number of stitches and rows per inch. If the gauge does not match the pattern, adjustments can be made by changing the needle size or adjusting tension.

Tension, also known as knitting or stitch tension, refers to the tightness or looseness with which a knitter works. It is a personal preference and can vary from person to person. Tension affects the overall appearance and drape of the knitted fabric. If a knitter's tension is too tight, the fabric may be stiff and rigid, while if it is too loose, the fabric may be loose and floppy. Achieving consistent tension is important, especially when working on larger projects or when multiple pieces need to be joined together.

Reading patterns is an essential skill for knitters, as it allows them to understand and follow instructions to create a specific design. Knitting patterns typically include a combination of written instructions, charts, and abbreviations. Written instructions provide step-by-step guidance on how to create each stitch and manipulate the yarn. Charts, on the other hand, use symbols and diagrams to represent stitches and their placement. Abbreviations are commonly used to condense instructions and make patterns more concise.

When reading a knitting pattern, it is important to pay attention to details such as stitch counts, shaping instructions, and any special techniques required. Understanding the terminology used in patterns is also crucial. For example, knit refers to creating a knit stitch, while purl refers to creating a purl stitch. Additionally, patterns often include information about the recommended yarn, needle size, and gauge.

In conclusion, understanding gauge, tension, and reading patterns is essential for successful knitting. By matching the gauge, achieving consistent tension, and accurately following pattern instructions, knitters can create beautiful and well-fitting garments and accessories. With practice and experience

Practicing Basic Stitches and Techniques with Mini Projects in Knitting: Practicing Basic Stitches and Techniques with Mini Projects in Knitting is a fantastic way to enhance your knitting skills and expand your repertoire of stitches. Whether you are a beginner or an experienced knitter, these mini projects provide the perfect opportunity to practice and perfect your technique.

One of the key benefits of working on mini projects is that they are quick and easy to complete. This means that you can focus on mastering specific stitches and techniques without committing to a large and time-consuming project. By breaking down the learning process into smaller, manageable tasks, you can build your confidence and gradually progress to more complex patterns.

When it comes to practicing basic stitches, mini projects offer a wide range of options. You can choose to work on projects that focus on specific stitches such as the knit stitch, purl stitch, or even more advanced stitches like cables or lace. By dedicating your time and attention to these stitches, you can refine your technique and ensure that your stitches are even and consistent.

In addition to practicing stitches, mini projects also allow you to experiment with different techniques. For example, you can try your hand at colorwork by knitting a small fair isle motif or explore the art of shaping by creating a mini hat or a pair of fingerless gloves. These projects not only provide a creative outlet but also help you understand how different techniques can be applied in various knitting projects.

Furthermore, mini projects are a great way to use up leftover yarn or try out new yarns. Since these projects require smaller amounts of yarn, you can easily use up those odd skeins that have been sitting in your stash. Additionally, you can experiment with different yarn weights and fibers, allowing you to discover new textures and effects in your knitting.

Finally, mini projects are perfect for gifting or adding a personal touch to your home. You can create adorable knitted toys, cozy mug cozies, or decorative dishcloths. These small projects not only showcase your knitting skills but also make thoughtful and heartfelt gifts for your loved ones.

In conclusion, practicing basic stitches and techniques with mini projects in knitting is a valuable and enjoyable way to improve your knitting skills. By dedicating your time to these smaller projects, you can focus on mastering specific stitches and techniques, experiment with different yarns, and create beautiful and functional items. So grab your needles, choose a mini project, and start knitting your way to knitting mastery!

Different Styles of Knit Blankets: There are various styles of knit blankets available, each offering a unique and distinct look. These styles range from traditional to modern, and can be made using different knitting techniques and patterns.

One popular style of knit blanket is the cable knit. Cable knitting involves creating intricate patterns using twisted stitches, resulting in a textured and visually appealing design. Cable knit blankets often feature bold and intricate cable patterns that add depth and dimension to the blanket. These blankets are not only cozy and warm, but also serve as a decorative element in any room.

Another style of knit blanket is the lace knit. Lace knitting involves creating delicate and intricate patterns using yarn overs and decreases. Lace knit blankets are known for their delicate and airy appearance, making them perfect for adding a touch of elegance to any space. These blankets are often made using lightweight yarns, making them ideal for warmer climates or as decorative throws.

Fair Isle knit blankets are another popular style. Fair Isle knitting involves using multiple colors of yarn to create intricate patterns and motifs. These blankets often feature geometric designs or traditional motifs, and are known for their vibrant and eye-catching appearance. Fair Isle knit blankets are a great way to add a pop of color and personality to any room.

For those looking for a more modern and minimalist style, there are also chunky knit blankets. These blankets are made using thick and bulky yarns, resulting in a cozy and plush texture. Chunky knit blankets are often made using oversized knitting needles or arm knitting techniques, creating a unique and trendy look. These blankets are perfect for snuggling up on a cold winter night or adding a touch of warmth and texture to a contemporary space.

In addition to these styles, there are countless other knit blanket designs and patterns to choose from. From traditional Aran knit blankets to intarsia knit blankets with intricate pictorial designs, the options are endless. Whether you prefer a classic and timeless look or a more modern and trendy style, there is a knit blanket out there to suit your taste and preferences.

Overall, knit blankets offer both functionality and style. They provide warmth and comfort, while also adding a decorative element to any space. With so many different styles and patterns to choose from, there is a knit blanket out there for everyone. So, whether you're looking to cozy up on a chilly evening or enhance the aesthetic of your home, consider adding a knit blanket to your collection.

Step-by-Step Guide to Knitting Your First Blanket:

Step 1: Gather all the necessary materials

Before you start knitting your first blanket, make sure you have all the materials you need. This includes knitting needles, yarn, a tapestry needle, and scissors. Choose a yarn that is suitable for a blanket, such as a bulky or super bulky weight yarn, as it will knit up faster and create a cozy and warm blanket.

Step 2: Choose a knitting pattern

Next, decide on the knitting pattern you want to use for your blanket. There are numerous patterns available, ranging from simple garter stitch to more intricate cable or lace patterns. If you're a beginner, it's best to start with a basic pattern that uses simple stitches. You can find free patterns online or in knitting books.

Step 3: Cast on stitches

Once you have your materials and pattern ready, it's time to cast on stitches. Casting on is the process of creating the first row of stitches on your knitting needle. The number of stitches you cast on will depend on the size of the blanket you want to make. Follow the instructions in your pattern to cast on the correct number of stitches.

Step 4: Start knitting

With your stitches cast on, you can now start knitting. Follow the pattern instructions for each row, knitting or purling as required. Take your time and make sure to keep your tension even throughout your knitting. This will ensure that your blanket has a consistent appearance.

Step 5: Continue knitting until desired length

Continue knitting rows according to your pattern until your blanket reaches the desired length. This may take some time, especially if you're making a large blanket. Knitting a blanket is a great project to work on while watching TV or relaxing in the evenings.

Step 6: Bind off stitches

Once your blanket has reached the desired length, it's time to bind off your stitches. Binding off is the process of finishing the edge of your knitting and securing the stitches so they don't unravel. Follow the instructions in your pattern to bind off your stitches.

Step 7: Weave in loose ends

After binding off, you will have loose ends of yarn that need to be woven in. Use a tapestry needle to carefully weave the loose ends into the back of your knitting. This will ensure that your blanket looks neat and tidy.

Step 8: Block your blanket (optional)

Blocking is a process that involves wetting your finished knitting and shaping it to the desired dimensions.

Exploring Colors, Textures, and Patterns in Blanket Making in Knitting: Blanket making in knitting offers a wide range of opportunities for exploring colors, textures, and patterns. With the ability to choose from an extensive palette of yarn colors, knitters can create visually stunning blankets that reflect their personal style and taste. Whether you prefer bold and vibrant hues or subtle and muted tones, the possibilities are endless.

Textures play a crucial role in blanket making, as they add depth and interest to the finished piece. Knitters can experiment with different stitch patterns, such as cables, lace, or bobbles, to create unique textures that enhance the overall design. By combining different stitch patterns or alternating between smooth and textured sections, knitters can create visually dynamic blankets that are both visually appealing and cozy to the touch.

Patterns are another exciting aspect of blanket making in knitting. From classic designs like stripes or chevron to more intricate motifs like Fair Isle or intarsia, there is a pattern to suit every knitter's skill level and aesthetic preferences. Patterns can be used to create focal points or to add visual interest throughout the blanket. They can also be combined with different colors and textures to create truly one-of-a-kind blankets that showcase the knitter's creativity and craftsmanship.

In addition to the creative possibilities, blanket making in knitting also offers practical benefits. Knitted blankets are known for their warmth and durability, making them perfect for snuggling up on chilly nights or for adding a cozy touch to any room. The process of knitting a blanket can also be a therapeutic and relaxing activity, allowing knitters to unwind and express their creativity while creating something beautiful and functional.

Whether you are a beginner knitter looking to explore the world of blanket making or an experienced knitter seeking new challenges, the world of colors, textures, and patterns in knitting offers endless opportunities for creativity and self-expression. So grab your knitting needles, choose your favorite yarns, and embark on a journey of exploration and discovery as you create your own unique and beautiful knitted blankets.

Understanding Sweater Construction and Sizing in Knitting:

Knitting a sweater can be a rewarding and fulfilling project for any knitting enthusiast. However, it can also be a daunting task, especially for beginners who are not familiar with sweater construction and sizing. In order to successfully knit a sweater that fits well and looks great, it is important to have a good understanding of these two key aspects.

Sweater construction refers to the way a sweater is put together, including the different parts and how they are joined. There are several common types of sweater constructions, each with its own unique characteristics. The most basic type is the seamless construction, where the sweater is knit in one piece, from the top down or from the bottom up. This type of construction eliminates the need for sewing or seaming, making it a popular choice for beginners. Another common construction method is the raglan, where diagonal lines are created from the neckline to the underarm, giving the sweater a distinctive look. Other types of constructions include set-in sleeves, drop shoulders, and saddle shoulders, each with its own advantages and challenges.

When it comes to sizing, it is important to understand that knitting patterns usually provide a range of sizes to accommodate different body types. These sizes are typically based on standard measurements, such as bust, waist, and hip circumference, as well as sleeve and body length. It is crucial to take accurate measurements of your own body before starting a sweater project, as this will help you choose the correct size and make any necessary adjustments to ensure a good fit. Keep in mind that different knitting patterns may have different ease options, which refers to the amount of extra room in the garment. Understanding ease and how it affects the fit of a sweater is essential for achieving the desired look and comfort.

In addition to construction and sizing, there are other factors to consider when knitting a sweater. Yarn choice is crucial, as different yarns have different properties and will affect the drape, warmth, and overall appearance of the finished garment. It is important to choose a yarn that is suitable for the intended purpose of the sweater, whether it is for everyday wear or special occasions. Gauge, or the number of stitches and rows per inch, is another important consideration. Achieving the correct gauge is crucial for ensuring that the sweater will fit as intended and that the stitch pattern will look as expected.

Overall, understanding sweater construction and sizing in knitting is essential for successfully completing a sweater project. By familiarizing yourself with different construction

Tips and Tricks for Knitting a Comfortable, Well-Fitting Sweater: Knitting a comfortable and well-fitting sweater requires attention to detail and a few helpful tips and tricks. Whether you are a beginner or an experienced knitter, these guidelines will ensure that your sweater turns out just the way you want it.

Firstly, it is essential to choose the right yarn for your sweater. Consider the fiber content, weight, and texture of the yarn. Natural fibers like wool or cotton are great choices as they provide warmth and breathability. Additionally, the weight of the yarn should match the pattern you are using. Thicker yarns create bulkier sweaters, while thinner yarns result in lighter garments. Lastly, the texture of the yarn can add visual interest to your sweater, so choose one that complements your style.

Next, take accurate measurements of your body before starting the project. This step is crucial to ensure a well-fitting sweater. Measure your bust, waist, hips, and arm length. Compare these measurements to the sizing chart provided in the pattern or use them to create a custom pattern. Remember to account for ease, which is the amount of extra room you want in your sweater. Negative ease creates a snug fit, while positive ease allows for a looser, more relaxed fit.

When knitting the sweater, pay attention to gauge. Gauge refers to the number of stitches and rows per inch in your knitting. It is crucial to match the gauge specified in the pattern to achieve the correct size and fit. Use the recommended needle size and yarn weight to obtain the correct gauge. If your gauge is off, adjust your needle size accordingly. Swatching is a great way to test your gauge before starting the actual sweater. It may seem tedious, but it will save you from potential disappointment later on.

To ensure a comfortable fit, consider incorporating shaping techniques into your sweater. Techniques like increases, decreases, and short rows can help create a flattering silhouette. For example, adding waist shaping can give your sweater a more tailored look. Additionally, consider the length of the sweater. If you prefer a longer or shorter length, make adjustments accordingly. Remember to try on the sweater as you go to ensure it fits well and make any necessary modifications.

Lastly, pay attention to finishing details. Blocking your sweater is essential to even out stitches and give it a polished look. Follow the blocking instructions provided in the pattern or use your preferred method. Additionally, consider adding ribbing or other edging techniques to the cuffs, hem, and neckline.

CHAPTER ONE

Introduction

Knitting is one of my favorites craft in winter in this book "Knitting Fundamentals for Beginners" I will be showing to you different knitting projects that are suitable for winter to live in comfort just be patient reading through all my instructional stages with photo guide on each stages. You can eventually start getting excited about wintry weather now that winter has arrived who doesn't love cozy nights blanket by using the hearth, wrapping up warm and frosty walks within the park and with it comes the threat to create a few seasonal DIY's.

I have been dreaming of outsized cozy blankets for a while now, having been inspired via worthy interiors filled with chunky knitted throws, so I determined to have a go at making my very own.

I will surely surprise you at how brief and smooth this DIY projects in this book will became to make and I love the result. If you will desire to make your personal projects; read carefully from the beginning of this book to the end to discover how I made my oversized arm knitted cozy blanket, winter sweater, lover spread sheet, scarf and other fantastic projects, then read through this book Stage by Stage thoroughly following each of my instructions.

CHAPTER TWO

DIY Craft patterns to make tassels and add to your knitting

There are several ways to make tassels to add in your knits whether you are making your very own knits, purchase them online from online shop or pick out them up from any craft shops, why no longer jazz them few person spirit, lead them to specific to you or personalize them for a gift. on this tutorial, Sandra Nesbitt of The female contact Designs shows you the way to make simple tassels, and the way tassels can upload a comfy, hippy vibe to your knits.

You may use your tassels at the tip of hooded jackets, the hem of ponchos, shawls or scarves. They appearance fantastic in the home too brought to the corners of cushions, throws and blankets and hanging from curtain ties and wall hangings.

When deciding on substances for your tassels, you can go together with a unique hand-dyed yarn selected specially to supplement your knit, upload a few ribbons, or if the knit you're embellishing is hand-crafted by way of a Folksy seller, you may even ask them in the event that they have any left-over yarn. For mini tasks like jewelry or a key ring, you can additionally make tassels from silk or cotton embroidery thread.

CHAPTER THREE

Tassel making instructional Guide

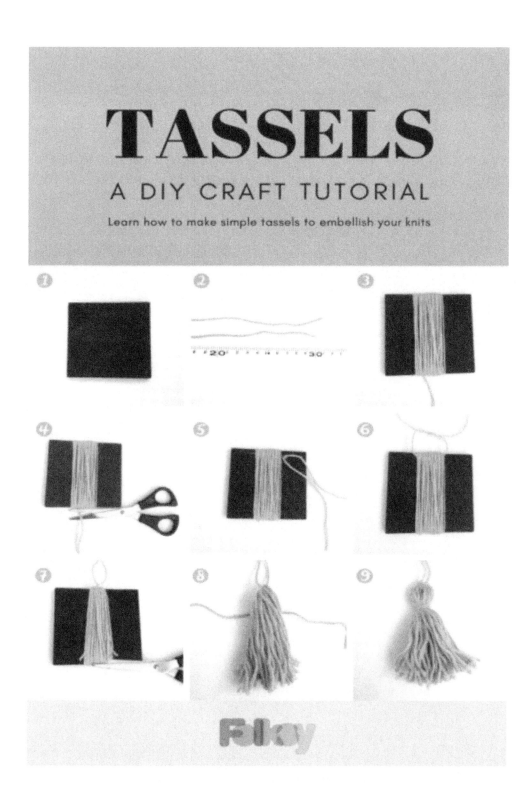

TASSELS

A DIY CRAFT TUTORIAL

Learn how to make simple tassels to embellish your knits

It is necessary to understand the ways to make simple tassels to decorate your knits on this simple Stage-by using-Stage.

1.   Reduce a piece of card to the favored period of your tassel.

2.   Reduce strands of wool 30cm lengthy.

3.   Wrap your wool round the card forty instances.

4.   Cut the wool.

5.   Thread one of the 30cm strands of wool via the top loops.

6.   Pull the two ends together and tie off (the strands may be utilized to connect the tassel in your knit).

7.   Reduce the loops at the lowest.

8.   Wind the second one 30cm strand round tassel 10cm from pinnacle four instances.

9.   Tie off tightly.

Stage-by way of-Stage instructions (with photos guide)

Stage 1: Cut a piece of card to the favored duration of your tassel.

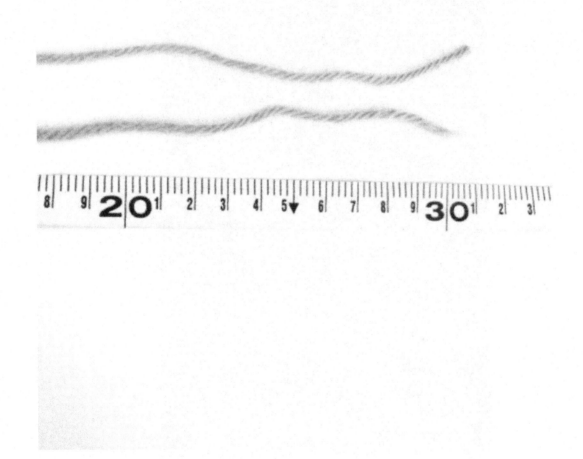

Stage 2: Reduce strands of wool 30cm lengthy.

Stage three: Now easily wrap your wool round the cardboard forty times completely.

Stage four: then cut the wool off.

Stage five: Then thread one of the 30cm strands of wool thru the pinnacle loops.

Stage 6: Also pull the 2 ends together and tie off (the strands may be utilized to connect the tassel for your knit along.

Stage 7: Just still cut the loops at the lowest.

Stage 8: Also wind the second one 30cm strand around tassel 10cm from top 4 times roll.

Stage nine: Then tie off tightly, now your tassel is prepared to enhance your knit (sew) easily

There are plenty of other methods to apply your tassels too and below are a few extra thoughts on how to use tassels from our proficient designers and makers on Folksy.

Purple Tassel and Pom Bag appeal Sea glass and Tassel jewelry Tassel embellishment for a hand-bound eBook Bag allure with Tassel Teal wine glass charm with tassel Beaded Bracelet with Tassel Crochet shawl with Tassel Fringe leather and Suede Tassel Key rings toddler Hat with Tassels Rose Gold Tassel Hoop jewelry

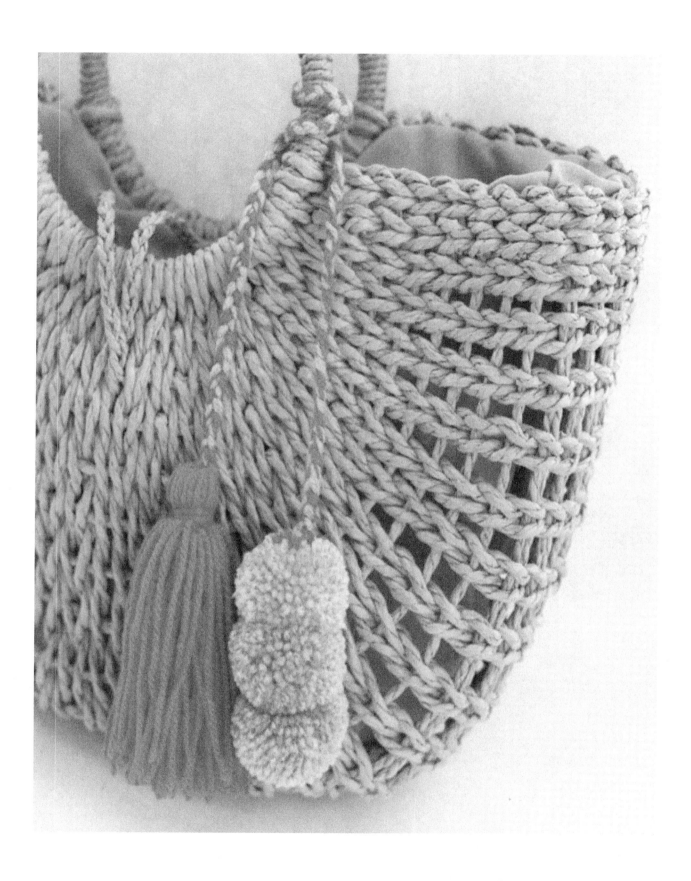

44

CHAPTER FOUR

Basic DIY knitting Stages for Beginners

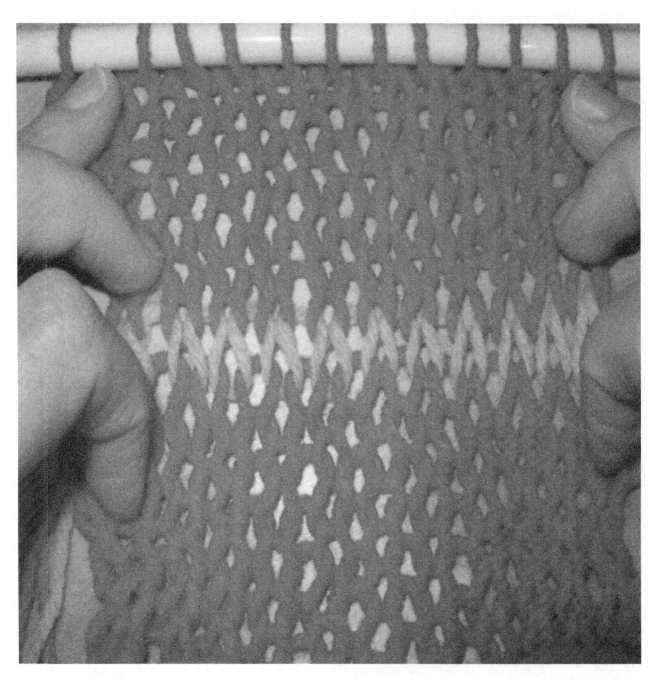

Understanding the basic knitting is one of the greatest common desire for many learning the knitting crafts and there are lots up in this book "knitting foundation for beginners" to now only a few addressing knitting. In this book I will be showing to you the fundamentals of knitting and is in no manner comprehensive however I have to get you started.

All you want to learn is some yarn and a couple of needles. In this I have utilized medium weight yarn and incredibly massive needles, so the interlocking loops would be clearer. Maximum knitting is achieved rather tighter than this.

Stage 1: A touch bit of idea

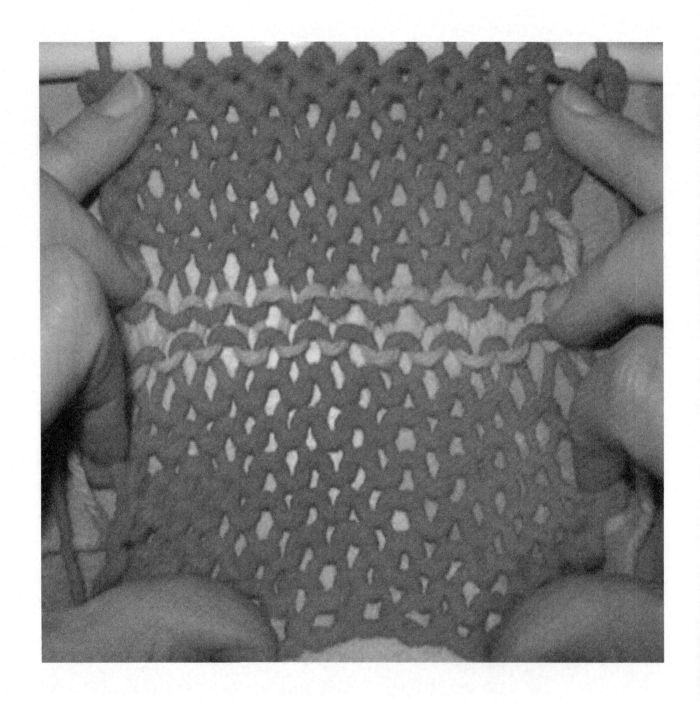

All that knitting surely is; a sequence of interlocking loops. Checking the front % once more, I utilized yellow thread in one row to make it simpler to peer how the loops interact. the second percent indicates the equal piece from the opposite aspect.

The primary P.C indicates the knit facet, and the second P.C suggests the purl side. A purl sew it is spelled with a u however stated much like pearl is exactly the same as a knit sew except it is worked from the alternative aspect. The smoother aspect that looks as if interlocking V's is going through you whilst you are knitting, and the bumpy facet that looks like interlocking united states is going through you when you purl.

In order to begin knitting, you will need to "solid on", or top off a knitting needle with starter loops. Then you may knit a few numbers of rows till the piece is the scale you want. Then you may "put off", or near out all of the loops so the knitting would not come unraveled once more.

There also are kinds of methods to preserve the needles and yarn. In this my knitting book I'm going to use of and discussing the Continental method, which essentially simply way the unfastened yarn give up is held within the left hand (percent three). This cease can also be held within the right hand, that is extra commonplace in the America however to my thoughts a bit less efficient.

Stage 2: Knitting On

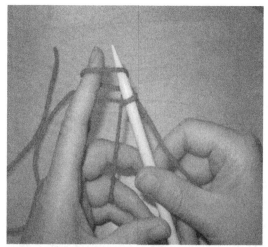

There are numerous specific methods to forge on and the one proven here is versatile and strong, even though not absolutely the most effective one which tends to get to the bottom of itself causing consternation, grief, and dropped stitches technique.

And for individuals who opt for text and static images begin with the aid of making a slip knot, leaving duration of yarn about three instances the completed width of your mission as a tail. put the slip knot on one needle, for your proper hand in case you're proper-passed I'm lefties you may attempt it this way or reverse it, whichever works for you and hold the long tail for your left hand, wrapping it around your first finger as in the first photo.

Next, slip the point of the needle under the loop on your finger, in order that each your finger and the needle are within the loop photographs 2 & three and along with your proper hand, grasp the yarn quit from the ball or skein, and bring it over the finger loop, between your finger and the needle and photos four, five, & 6 while protecting the right hand yarn piece down, slip the loop off your finger and over the end of the needle pics 7, eight, & nine. At this point pull lightly at the left-hand yarn give up to close up the loop, forcing the opposite yarn quit and held by means of your right hand to loop around the needle in photo 10 & 11.

At this point you now have to have two stitches for your needle, as the first slip knot counts because the first sew.

Retain this way till you have got sufficient stitches. For a studying swatch, 12 or 16 is plenty. I went loopy and ended up with 32!

Stage three: The Knit sew

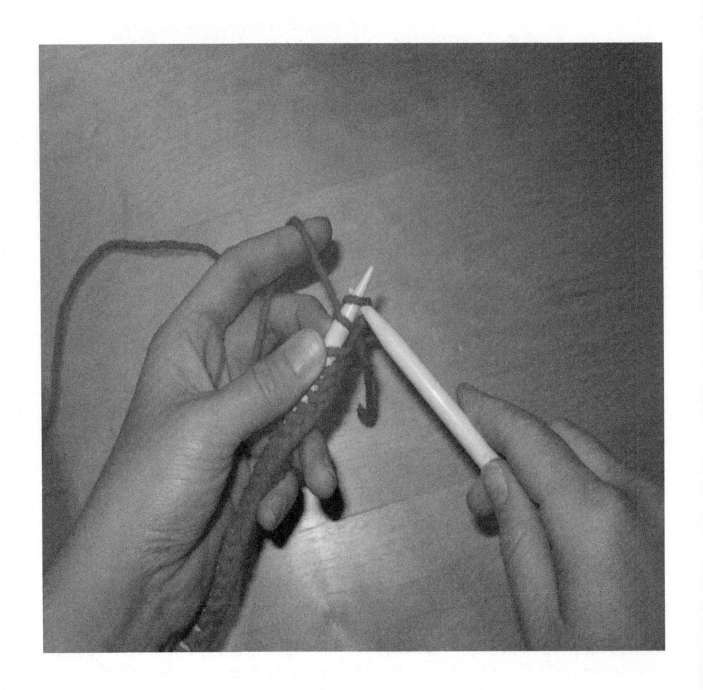

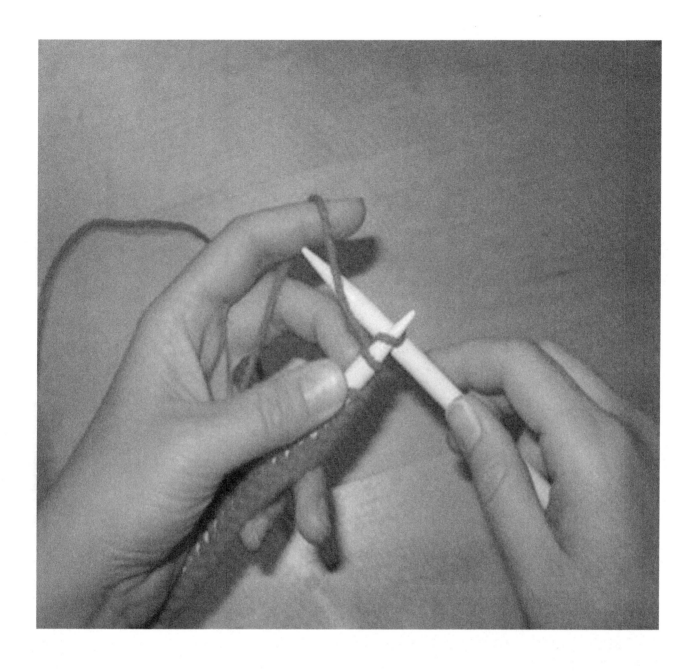

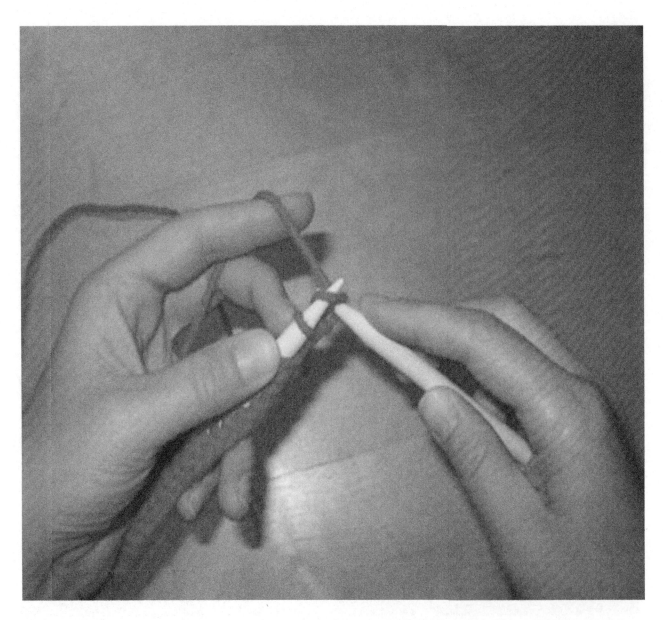

As I stated earlier, there are primary stitches in knitting, based on which direction you are pulling the yarn thru the loop in. One way is referred to as knitting; the alternative way is known as purling. When it really is full and the left needle is empty, transfer fingers.

Right in this chapter I will show to how to make a knit sew (stitch) while retaining the yarn to your left hand as shown. Wrap the tail of the yarn thru your palms in a few way that feels natural the intention is to hold it taut but not so tight which you cannot pull greater out as wanted and a few wrap it two times across the pinky.

Insert the right-hand needle thru the primary or next loop at the left needle pic 1 and along with your left forefinger, wrap the yarn across the proper needle counter-clockwise percent 2. You may also consider this as slipping the needle in the back of the yarn.

Preserving the yarn around the needle, deliver it lower back thru the primary loop, in order that the left hand's yarn comes through too photos three and four. It's less difficult to do than to describe!

Ultimately, slip the unique loop off the left needle, preserving the new loop at the right needle (% five). You've got made one knit stitch (sew).

Stage 4: The Purling

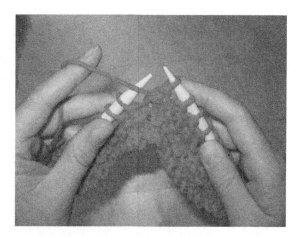
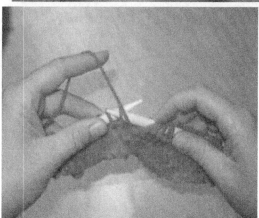

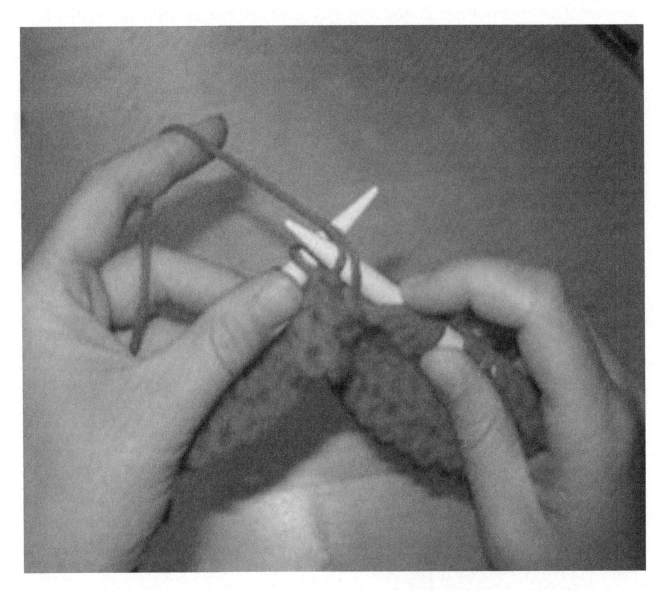

The purl stitch is the knit stitch, backwards. as opposed to starting from the front and pulling a loop from the again of the paintings via to the front, you begin from the returned and pull a loop via from the front.

A pic 1 suggests the position of the left-hand yarn, in the front of the work. From this function, insert the right-hand needle from the back of the work toward you via the sew at the left-hand needle photographs 2 and 3.

Now wrap the yarn around the needle counter-clockwise, or up over the needle and round to the left (snap shots 3 & four). Trap the yarn with the end of the right needle and pull it thru the loop (snap shots 5, 6 & 7). It helps in this manouevre to tilt the left needle tip in the direction of you.

Subsequently, slip the vintage loop off the left needle; keeping the only you pulled via it on the right needle (pix 8 & nine). You've got completed a purl sews your pic 10.

Stage five: getting rid of

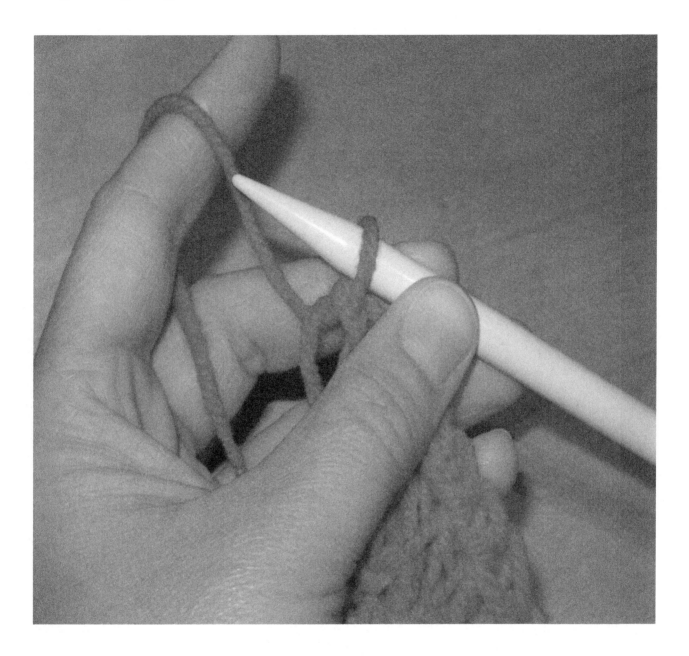

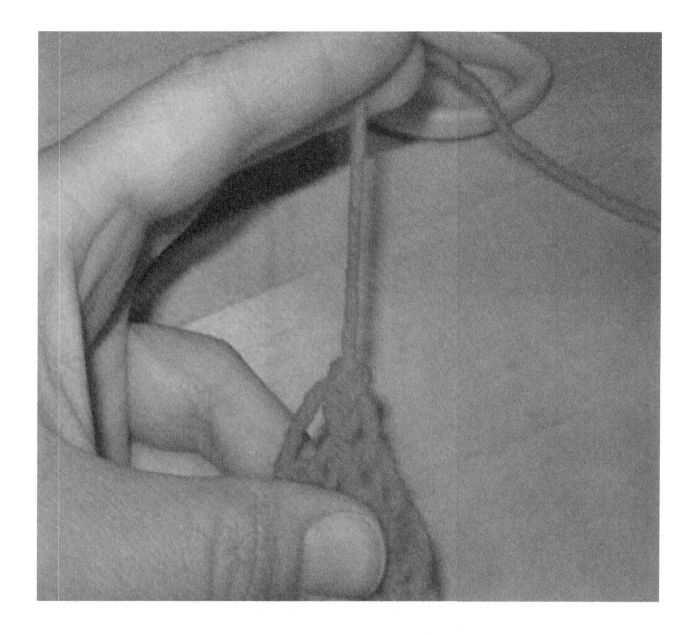

So that you've to knit and purled and knitted and also purled and you're done. How do you forestall, without leaving all the ones loops unfastened to be unraveled?

I unaccountably overlooked taking images of all but the final stitch; I can try to redo them quickly.

When you're equipped to eliminate, maintain the paintings as if you had been going to knit another row. Knit (knit is a bit easier than purl however you could do away with purl-wise too) one stitch. Slip that stitch again onto the left-hand needle. Now, knit one greater sew, however instead of sticking the proper needle through simply the ultimate stitch on the left needle, stick it via - the one you slipped onto it and the one past. Pull the loop through each stitch. You presently have one stitch at the right needle, but you've got made two knits - see how this is going paintings the complete width on this way. On the cease, you will have one sew ultimate. Reduce your yarn and pull the cut end via this loop to fasten it, and pull tight. Pix are of this last loop)

Stage 6: more Stuff

Basic beneficial phrases:

•   Garter stitch: while you knit a row, and turn and knit once more, instead of purling. This makes a crosswise ribbing that has numerous vertical stretches and the primary % indicates a few rows of garter sew.

•   Stockinet stitch: while you knit a row, and turn after which purl a row and most things are made this manner, it's were given all the knit-searching stitches one aspect and all the purl-searching stitches on the alternative.

•   Ribbing: A vertical alternation of knits and purls normally found on the edges of sweaters - wrist, hem, neckline. I don't have an image of this yet however you in all likelihood have examples around the house.

•   Dropped sew: that is in reality a mistake, when you slip a sew off the left-facet needle without already having pulled some other loop thru it. if you word you have done this, prevent and go back to restore it as it will purpose a run, or ladder - it's going to resolve a row all the way down.

•   Reducing: the overall case of putting off. Generally that is utilized whilst you do not want to complete off all of the stitches, but just a few, as when you're running a curved facet like a neckline.

Congratulation pure Knitting

CHAPTER FIVE

DIY stage by stage knitting of winter cozy blankets

It was an exciting knitting moment knitting in winter start getting excited about winter weather now that winter has arrived who doesn't love cozy nights blanket by using the hearth, wrapping up warm and frosty walks within the park and with it comes the threat to create a few seasonal DIY's.

I have been dreaming of outsized blankets for a while now, having been inspired via worthy interiors filled with chunky knitted throws, so I determined to have a go at making my very own.

I was surely surprised at how brief and smooth this DIY became to make and I love the result. If you need to make your personal read directly to discover how I made my oversized arm knitted blanket then read through this book Stage by Stage thoroughly.

I discovered this exceptional massive yarn on Betsy from Wool in a tender grey and purchased balls for £forty five. I best desired a medium blanket and become advocated that two would make a blanket around 25 x 50 inches (63x127cm). It is merino wool that means it is a lot softer and greater gentle for your skin than pure wool, which can be a little scratchy. I had in no way tried arm knitting before but idea I'd give it a move because it creates a adorable open knit, perfect for a chunky throw. Wool Couture threw in a free arm knitting tutorial with my order so I may want to start right away while my wool arrived. If you want to attempt arm knitting follow together with my Stage by Stage, all you need is some wool and your very personal palms.

 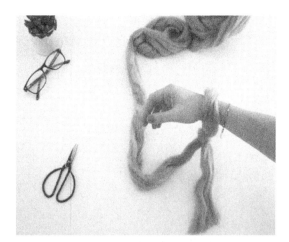

I begins out by using tying a loop in the end of the yarn and slipping it over my proper hand.

1. Using the knot under my wrist and palm dealing with me I laid the yarn from the back of my surrender to the front of my palm.

2. Using my left hand I then went via the loop underneath my wrist, ensuring the yarn nearest the ball was at the right facet of my left wrist.

3 & 4. I grabbed the yarn length and pulled lower back through the loop my left hand had come through, allowing the loop to slip off my right hand in doing so.

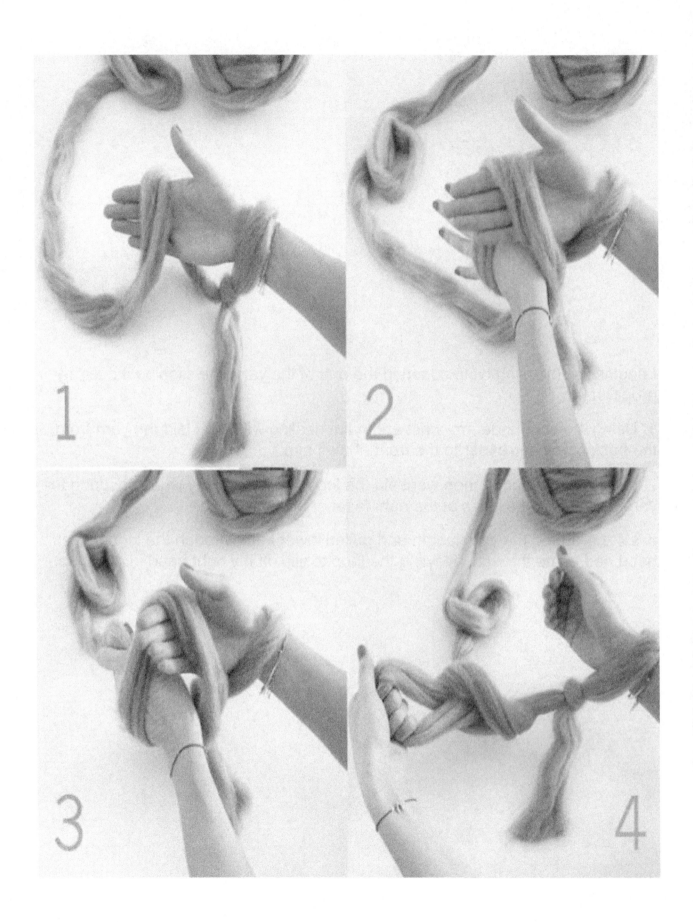

Using the loop I has simply made I located over my right wrist to create two stitches. I persevered Stages 1 to 4 till I had cast on sixteen stitches (as this is what Claire from cautioned on my right arm.

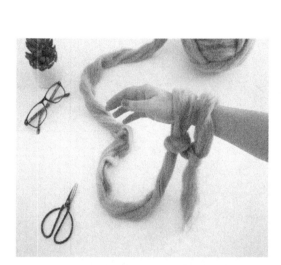

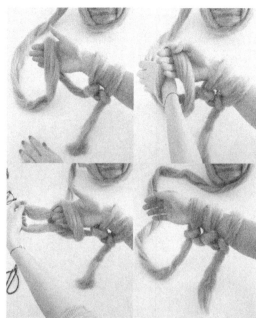

Working with first row

1. Firstly in order to start creating my first row I wrapped my yarn around the front of my right thumb and made a fist to preserve the yarn completely.

2. Then take the subsequent sew (knit) alongside, (3) I surpassed this over my fist and the yarn i was retaining.

4. I make a passed the loop that changed into in my proper fist over the left hand to create my first stitch of this row.

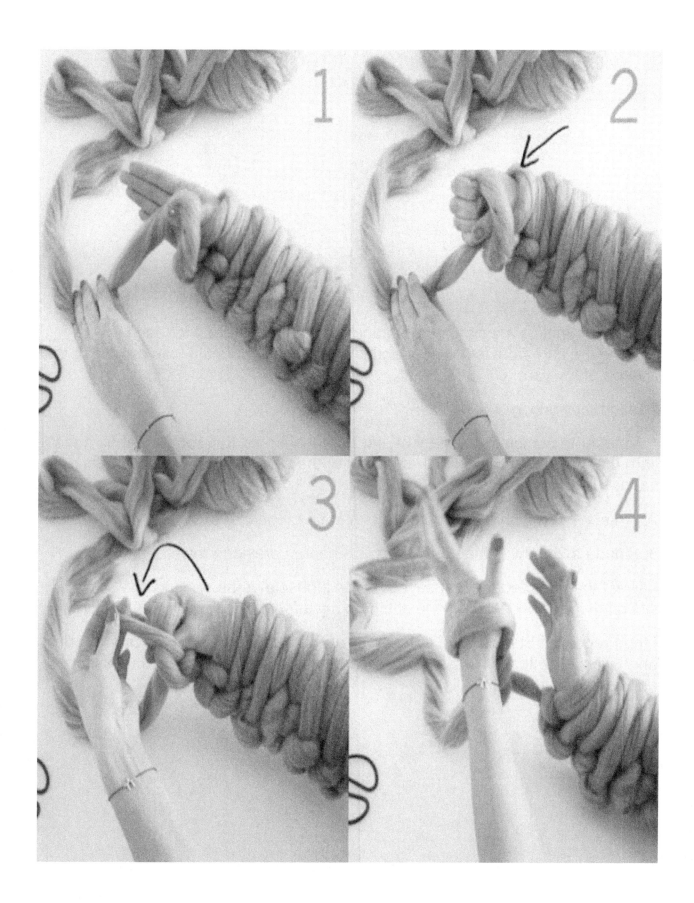

I started Stages 1: Four in this row till all the loops had been on my left arm and i had completed this row.

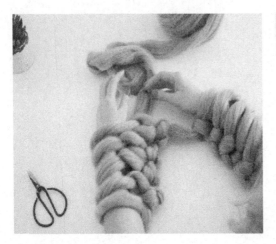 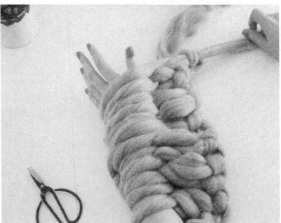

I also start knitting my blanket repeating the identical Stages for each row, passing the yarn from left to right and lower back again until I was coming to the give up of my yarn.

Casting off working

1. In order to complete my blanket and get rid of I started through grabbing the yarn duration in the equal fist that has all of the stitches on my right (proper) hand.

2. I made 1 sew within the equal way I had on preceding rows.

3. I made a 2d sew in the equal manner I had on previous rows.

4/five. I then handed the first sew over the pinnacle of the second one sew and slid off my left hand leaving one stitch on my left hand.

I then repeated Stages three to five until all stitches wherein off my proper arm and I was left with one loop and to finish I pulled the final yarn via the this loop and tied it off.

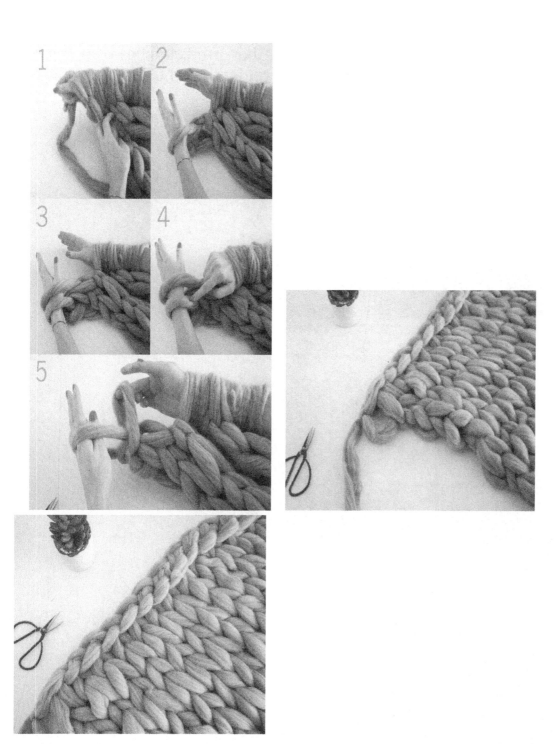

Expert guide: go away masses of yarn before disposing of and try and hold the stitches large a unfastened to keep away from making this row too tight.

Arm knitting takes a touch being utilized to and some is fiddling however as soon as I got the dangle of it I simply loved it. My blanket knitted up actually fast and that I had completed it within an hour or so. I gave my blanket a bit stretch and pull out to make the stitches even, before placing it on my bed. ultimately it measured about 40 x 40 inches, a touch greater than predicted however this become probably as i utilized to be arm knitting rather than the use of needles.

However, I love how snug and relaxed this throw is, the yarn is tremendous smooth and the proper coloration of grey for winter. My spare room is white on white, tender neutrals and copper highlights so I suppose it'll cross properly in there.

My first cross at arm knitting grew to become out certainly well and that i assume it is a extremely good venture for beginners looking to learn how to knit or people who need a quick mission to get into knitting. Wool Couture have a number of wool for any venture however additionally sell readymade blankets like mine in case you need to shop for one already made up and I take a look at them out here

I am hoping you've got loved this iciness hotter of an academic. Have you attempted or would you want to strive arm knitting

CHAPTER SIX

How to make an easy Knit Blanket

In order to create an easy knit blanket you must follow these instructions carefully stage by stage below;

Stage 1: make some choices

Determine what yarn you want to apply and the way loose you need your blanket to be.

Stage 2: Create a chain

First tie a knot on the quit of your yarn then make a loop about 1-three" away from the knot. Pull your working yarn thru the loop until you've created a 1.five-2" loop.

Repeat this procedure until you've got your desired quantity of hyperlinks. We did about 20 hyperlinks.

You may determine how many links you need based on the size of your loops. in case you need your blanket to be 40″ extensive and also you're the usage of 2″ loops, then you will want approximately twenty (20) chains.

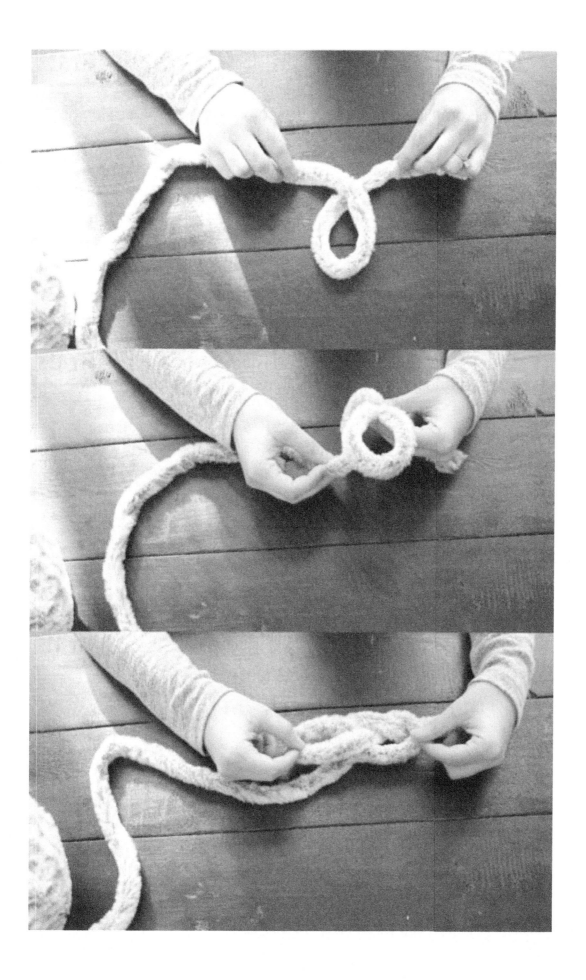

Stage 3: create a row of loops

This is the maximum complicated Stage of the complete blanket, so don't be discouraged if it's no longer as clean as you had been hoping.

For this Stage, you need to locate all the places that your knots "bump out." you'll slide your finger below the primary bump and pull your operating yarn thru to create your first loop.

Then locate the subsequent bump, slide your finger beneath it and pull your running yarn through to create every other loop. Retain down your chain until you have the desired number of loops.

Study: make sure that your loops are usually the equal size. Consistency in sizing is the most essential element for knitting a blanket. in case you are inconsistent for your loop sizes, your blanket will come to be being a funny shape and it will appearance sloppy. a few holes might be large, a few will be tight. pay attention most on making sure that each one of your loops are the identical length.

Stage 4: knit your first real row

You're going to disregard the first loop in this row for now and simply flow onto the second one loop. Pull your working yarn thru the backside of the loop to create a new loop.

Make sure that loop stays in vicinity whilst you circulate onto the following loop and pull the running yarn thru. Maintain going till you attain the end of your row.

Completing a row

Keep in mind how you omitted the primary loop as well now it might look like you've got an ungainly loop placing out on the aspect.

You're going to deal with this awkward aspect loop as if it had been any other loop. simply pull your working yarn thru the backside and create a new loop with it.

Now your loop must appear like it belongs to the same row as your other loops in place of being an awkward aspect loop.

Starting a brand new row

While you start a new row, you're going to bypass over the loop which you just created with the operating yarn and the awkward side loop. Once you pass the loop you simply created in Stage five, simply repeat Stage four until you get to the other facet.

Stage four: repeat until you're nearly performed

In case you're running with the Sherpa yarn, you need to be mainly careful that no loops get skipped. Because the yarn is so smooth, it slips without difficulty.

If you finish your blanket and discover which you missed a few loops, stitch them to some other loop to save you your blanket from unraveling.

Connecting two yarn skeins

When you run out of yarn and need to attach a brand new one, it's quite simple. genuinely tie the 2 pieces of yarn collectively with a knot.

While I utilized to be creating the Sherpa Yarn blanket, I utilized a double knot since the fabric comes undone so without problems. Don't fear approximately the knot–the yarn is so soft which you shouldn't note it.

Stage 5: Make the completing row

You'll want excess yarn for this Stage, so forestall knitting your blanket when you have sufficient yarn to do 1.five-three rows final. What you're going to do is loop the primary loops round your hand (don't forget about the first loop such as you commonly could).

Then pull your working yarn through the ones loops to create a new loop. keep this loop in your hand and upload the next loop within the row to your hand. Pull the running yarn through to create a brand new loop. Preserve repeating until you get all the manner to the end. Don't neglect to grab the awkward aspect loop too.

After you pull the yarn via the awkward side loop, you recognize that there is still an extra loop. Then take hold of your running yarn and weave it through the loop and pull until the blanket is tight. For the Sherpa Yarn blanket, I introduced an additional double knot on the stop simply for added safety.

At this point you weave in any excess yarn which you would possibly as you have. We needed to weave inside the yarn that was leftover from the final row as well as the extra yarn from the primary row.

You probably did it I told you the technique turned into smooth. The hardest element is staying consistent with the loops sizes, but when you try this, you're nicely to your way to becoming a knit blanket seasoned and feel unfastened to attain out with any questions.

THANKS FOR READING

Printed in Great Britain
by Amazon